END TIMES

A STUDY OF PROPHECY

VERSE BY VERSE MINISTRY
INTERNATIONAL

TEACHING THE WHOLE COUNSEL OF GOD

twitter.com/VBVMinistry

facebook.com/vbvmi

instagram.com/versebyverse_

Watch us on YouTube

CREDITS

—————○—————

STUDY AUTHORS
Teaching by Stephen Armstrong
Workbook by Houston Heflin, EdD

EDITING
Jeanette Cameron, Risen Editing

WORKBOOK LAYOUT & GRAPHIC DESIGN
Drew Rodgers

VIDEO PRODUCER
Randy Schnedler

CAMERA OPERATORS
Rob Hain
Randy Schnedler
Trevor Schnedler

PRODUCTION ASSISTANCE
Aware Productions

OHC PRODUCTION TEAM
Marty Hill, Producer
Rob Striffler, Audio
Deron Means, Audio
Richard Mendiola, Camera Operator
Ronnie Price, Camera Operator
Dan Oliver, Camera Operator

GUEST APPEARANCE
Max Lucado

ACKNOWLEDGEMENTS

We are grateful for the many friends and supporters of our ministry who made this teaching series possible. In particular, the ministry wishes to acknowledge the following individuals:

Joe Baumgartner, VBVMI Board member, for managing the details of this project and ensuring its completion.

Kathryn Bashaw, VBVMI Operations Director, for coordinating and managing the many details of this complex project.

The staff and volunteers of Oak Hills Church, San Antonio, for hosting the VBVMI End Times event with open arms and open hearts.

The VBVMI Board of Directors, staff, family, friends, proofreaders, and the technical production team who made this project possible.

Pastor Armstrong would also like to thank the following individuals:

His wife and partner of 29 years, Annette, for her many years of patient, loving support and guidance, without which this project and VBVMI ministry would not exist.

Max Lucado, Minster of Preaching of Oak Hills Church, for his friendship, encouragement, and guidance.

Brian Smith for his years of friendship, counsel, and support in leading VBVMI for the glory of Christ.

INTRODUCTION

———————○———————

This study was created to help you, your class, or small group understand more about the *end times*. You may have heard this topic called *eschatology*, but we will be using the term end times. To help you in your study, we will look at Revelation, Daniel, and some of the New Testament letters. These Scriptures will help you understand what the Bible has to say about what has been, what is, and what will come.

A CONTROVERSIAL TOPIC

We want to acknowledge from the beginning that this is an area of study that has some controversy associated with it. There are a lot of disagreements within the church about what the Bible has to say about this important topic. Regardless of our perspective of this topic, followers of Jesus can still agree on the most important things.

THE GOOD NEWS OF THE GOSPEL

Jesus is God's Son, He is the way to the Father, and He is the Savior of the world. Through faith in Jesus we are given the great gifts of forgiveness and eternal life with God. The sins that separate us from God and harm our relationships with others are forgiven through the sacrifice of Jesus, who died on the cross, was buried, and rose again on the third day. He overcame death and invites His disciples to follow Him, not only in how we live our lives on earth, but also in how we will overcome death to live forever in heaven. These are all things we have been told and can be sure of (see John 3:16; Acts 4:12; Romans 5:10, 10:9).

STUDYING FOR WISDOM AND GUIDANCE

Christians are far less in agreement about details of Christ's return, yet understanding His second coming and other questions of the end times is still important. Our prayer for you is this material will guide you to greater understanding of Scripture and greater anticipation of the Lord's fulfillment of His promises. We are confident the Holy Spirit will teach you as you pursue Christ in the Scriptures, and Verse By Verse Ministry International stands ready to assist you in your journey of discovering the full counsel of God's Word.

LEARNING OBJECTIVES

It's helpful to have an idea of where you would like to go before setting off on a journey. In that spirit we've created a few overarching goals for participants in this study.

Our goals for you in this study are:

1. To obtain a foundational knowledge of the Bible's teaching on end times;
2. To gain confidence in your ability to understand biblical prophecy;
3. To grow in your relationship with Jesus through a study of His Word;
4. And to live a more Christ-like life in response to what you learn.

OUTLINE OF LESSONS

Each lesson follows the same format consisting of these eight sections:

 PRAYER: Begin every lesson with prayer, inviting God to open your eyes, ears, and hearts to see what He wants to teach you through His Word.

 REVIEW: Discuss a few review questions as you begin so you or your group can recall what you've already learned as a foundation for new learning.

 VIDEO: Watch the video provided for each lesson. Each video is about twenty minutes long.

 DISCUSSION: Record your observations and share them with your group (if applicable). You may not have time to cover every question, so focus on the questions that most interest you or your group.

 APPLICATION: Each lesson leads to application. We want you and your group to find yourself in the text by appreciating how the Bible is offering guidance for your life.

 PRAYER: End your study time in prayer, thanking the Lord for His Word and any insights you were given in that day's lesson. Ask the Lord for the faith and courage to follow Jesus and to live out what you have learned.

 HOMEWORK: Optional homework tasks are provided if you want to study in more depth before the next lesson.

 ADDITIONAL RESOURCES: We offer references to more study materials available from our comprehensive online study library at vbvmi.org.

OVERVIEW OF LESSONS

LESSON 1
The Structure of Revelation
Outline and Interpretation (Rev. 1:19)

📺 **Video 1 (13:22)**

LESSON 2
The Church Age and the Seven Letters
The Seven Letters (Rev. 2–3)

📺 **Video 2 (18:36)**

LESSON 3
The Great Apostasy
The Great Apostasy (Rev. 3;
2 Thess. 2; 1 Tim. 4; 2 Tim. 3)

📺 **Video 3 (22:26)**

LESSON 4
Understanding God's Timeline
Ages and Last Days

📺 **Video 4 (13:03)**

LESSON 5
The Age of the Gentiles (Daniel 2 and 7)
Purpose for the Age of Gentiles
(Lev. 26; Deut. 29; Deut. 30)

📺 **Video 5 (17:28)**

LESSON 6
The Seventy Sevens (Daniel 9)
The Final Seven

📺 **Video 6 (25:09)**

LESSON 7
Signs of the Times
Events Prior to Daniel's Final Seven

📺 **Video 7 (10:56)**

LESSON 8
The End of the Age
Signs of the End of the Age (Olivet
Discourse—Matt. 24)

📺 **Video 8 (35:04)**

LESSON 9
**The Resurrection of the Bride
(Rev. 4–5; 1 Thess. 1, 5; 1 Cor. 15)**
The Jewish Wedding Tradition

📺 **Video 9 (21:41)**

LESSON 10
The Departure of Christ
The Reason for Jesus's Departure
(Luke 13)
The Messianic Miracle
The Unforgivable Sin

📺 **Video 10 (22:39)**

LESSON 11
The Return of Christ
The Covenants with Israel

📺 **Video 11 (12:42)**

LESSON 12
The Saving of Israel
Armageddon
The Saving of Israel

📺 **Video 12 (25:10)**

INSTRUCTIONS FOR STUDENTS

If you are studying in a small group, your group leader/facilitator will determine how you will use this material. Depending on meeting length, group interests, and other factors, your leader may skip some sections of each lesson, assign homework, or make other changes to suit your group's needs. Nevertheless, we encourage all students to read through every question, especially in the Application section.

ACCESSING END-TIMES VIDEOS

Part of each group meeting time is devoted to viewing a short teaching video featuring Stephen Armstrong. This video is an essential part of each lesson. All videos are available via streaming over the Internet at www.vbvmiendtimesstudy.org as well as in the Videos section of the VBVMI website (www.vbvmi.org/videos). Videos are also available for viewing through our mobile apps and on the VBVMI AppleTV app.

If you have access to a reliable internet connection at your group meeting location, we recommend connecting a laptop computer, tablet, or smartphone directly to a larger screen (i.e., a TV) and streaming the videos from the Internet during class time.

In cases where an Internet connection is not available, you may download the videos to your device ahead of time. Then simply play each week's video using the copy stored on your device. (Please note all videos are protected by copyright and are free for viewing and distribution but may not be sold or altered.)

In cases where it is not possible to view the videos during class time, we recommend students view each week's video before the class meeting. Use the additional meeting time for the Review, Discussion, and Application sections.

ADDITIONAL SUPPORT

While the *End Times Group Study* curriculum was designed for groups, it can also be used by individual students working alone. Obviously, individual students can't participate in group discussion or ask questions, so our ministry offers online support for answering your questions and connecting you with other students. Please visit the *End Time Group Study* website (www.vbvmiendtimesstudy.org) for more information.

The VBVMI website (www.vbvmi.org) also offers helpful resources and supplemental materials to aid in your study. In particular, we offer a complete verse-by-verse study of the book of Revelation, which is a great resource for those desiring a deeper study of eschatology.

Should you need additional help during your study, you may submit questions to VBVMI through our website or by email at letters@versebyverseministry.org.

INSTRUCTIONS FOR LEADERS

We've designed this 12-week group study especially for Bible study groups, Sunday school classes, life groups, and other small group meetings. Each weekly lesson directs students through a series of activities that can be accomplished in as little as one hour. Students are not required to study outside the group meeting, though optional homework is available for those seeking a more challenging study.

This curriculum is adaptable to different group needs and leadership styles. Depending on the length of your meeting time, group size, and spiritual needs of your students, you may vary the time devoted to each part of a lesson. For example, some leaders may choose to follow our format closely by answering every question, while other leaders may decide to skip some questions in favor of more discussion time.

Therefore, we encourage leaders to use our materials in whatever way best suits the needs and interests of your study group.

ACCESSING END-TIMES VIDEOS

Part of each group meeting time is devoted to viewing a short teaching video featuring Stephen Armstrong. This video is an essential part of each lesson. All videos are available via streaming over the Internet at www.vbvmiendtimesstudy.org as well as in the Videos section of the VBVMI website (www.vbvmi.org/videos). Videos are also available for viewing through our mobile apps and on the VBVMI AppleTV app.

If you have access to a reliable Internet connection at your group meeting location, we recommend connecting a laptop computer, tablet, or smartphone directly to a larger screen (i.e., a TV) and streaming the videos from the Internet during class time.

In cases where an Internet connection is not available, you may download the videos to your device ahead of time. Then simply play each week's video using the copy stored on your device. (Please note all videos are protected by copyright and are free for viewing and distribution but may not be sold or altered.)

In cases where it is not possible to view the videos during class time, we recommend students view each week's video before the class meeting. Use the additional meeting time for the Review, Discussion, and Application sections.

ADDITIONAL SUPPORT

The VBVMI website (www.vbvmi.org) offers helpful resources and supplemental materials to aid in your group study. In particular, we offer a complete verse-by-verse study of the book of Revelation, which is a great resource for students desiring a deeper study of eschatology.

Should you need additional help in answering students' questions during your study, you may submit questions to VBVMI through our website or by email at letters@versebyverseministry.org.

RECOMMENDED TIME FOR GROUPS

SECTION	60-Min. Meeting	90+ Min. Meeting	COMMENTS
PRAYER	1 Min.	>2 Min.	Select a willing individual to pray on behalf of the entire group.
REVIEW	<5 Min.	>10 Min.	Can be eliminated in favor of giving time to other sections.
VIDEO	13-35 Min.	13-35 Min.	All videos can be found at www.vbvmiendtimesstudy.org. On weeks with longer videos, reduce or eliminate the Review section. On weeks with shorter videos, allocate extra time to Discussion or Application.
DISCUSSION	<20 Min.	>30 Min.	Cover as many questions as desired, focusing on those that generate the most interest in your group.
APPLICATION	<10 Min.	>20 Min.	Application questions can be covered in the group time or assigned as homework.
PRAYER	2 Min.	>6 Min.	If more group prayer time is desired, reduce or eliminate the Review section.
HOMEWORK	Varies	Varies	Homework is optional. If a leader assigns homework weekly, substitute a Homework Review time for the normal Review section each week.

LESSON 1

The Structure of Revelation

LEARNING OBJECTIVES: Your goal is to...

1. Understand the structure of Revelation;
2. Evaluate both John's reaction to Jesus in Revelation 1 and your own reaction to Jesus;
3. And begin studying Revelation with a framework for understanding the book.

PRAYER

Thank God for the gift of the Bible and ask God to teach you through this amazing gift. In your quiet time, reflect on the power of God's Word to change the way you live your life.

REVIEW

1. Why are you interested in studying the end times? What is most interesting to you about this topic?

_____

_____

_____

_____

_____

_____

_____

_____

_____

_____

2. What goals do you have for this study? Is there any special knowledge or understanding you're pursuing about this topic? Are there any questions you're hoping will be answered through this study?

_____

_____

_____

_____

_____

_____

VIDEO 1
The Structure of Revelation
Outline and Interpretation
(Rev. 1:19)

All videos are available for viewing or download at:
vbvmiendtimesstudy.org

DISCUSSION

1. How would you summarize the major points you learned from the video?

_____

_____

_____

_____

_____

_____

_____

2. Why is **Revelation 1:19** so important to understanding the book of Revelation?

_____

_____

_____

_____

_____

_____

_____

_____

_____

_____

3. The book of Revelation is broken down into three parts. How does knowing this help your interpretation of the book?

      Things John saw = chapter 1 (these are things John saw)
      Things that are = chapters 2–3 (dictations of seven letters)
      Things after these things = chapters 4–22 (visions John sees)

Take just two minutes to skim through the book of Revelation and notice the distinctions in the sections identified by this outline.

_____

_____

_____

_____

_____

_____

_____

4. Review **Revelation chapter 1** together (or read if you have time). Notice how John's encounter with Jesus is different from his experience with Jesus on earth. What impact does this have on John's understanding of prophecy?

5. In **Revelation 1:17** John's response as he encounters Jesus is to drop to the ground in fear. The most frequent instruction by angels as they introduce themselves throughout the Bible is "Do not be afraid." Something about the presence of angelic beings startles people and causes an instinctive reaction of fear. Consider the examples from Scripture below. Why do you think human beings feel fear in the presence of angels?

"When Zechariah saw the angel he was startled and gripped with fear. But the angel said to him: 'Do not be afraid, Zechariah'" (Luke 1:13).

"Mary was greatly troubled... but the angel said to her, 'Do not be afraid, Mary'" (Luke 1:30).

"The shepherds were terrified, but the angel said to them, 'Do not be afraid'" (Luke 2:10).

6. Proverbs 9:10 says, "The fear of the Lord is the beginning of wisdom, and knowledge of the Holy One is understanding." Do you understand *fear* in these verses to mean "being afraid," "respect," "awe," "true love," "admiration," or something else?

"The shepherds were terrified, but the angel said to them, 'Do not be afraid'" *Luke 2:10*.

APPLICATION

1. John was given a vision to observe what God had done and was going to do. What work(s) of God has He revealed to you in your life? Where or how have you seen God working?

2. In **Revelation 1** John encountered Jesus in a new way. What encounters or experiences with God have led you to a new perspective on God or God's identity? How have you come to see God in a new way? Have you ever been surprised by God?

3. Understanding what God is doing in the present can be more difficult than recognizing His work in the past. Consider for a moment what God might be doing currently in your life. Do you see Him at work around you today in some specific way? Or can you testify to His past work?

4. Two times in **Revelation chapter 1** God is described as preexistent, existing, and ongoing. In other words, God was in the past, God is in the present, and God will be in the future. Consider these two verses:

> "Grace and peace to you from Him who is, and who was, and who is to come" **Rev. 1:4**.

> "The Almighty is, and was, and is to come" **Rev. 1:8.**

Why do you think it was important for John (the author of Revelation) to emphasize God's eternal existence in chapter 1?

_____

_____

_____

_____

_____

_____

_____

_____

_____

5. How do these descriptions of God's (and Jesus's) eternal nature give you confidence or hope?

_____

_____

_____

_____

_____

_____

 **PRAYER**

Thank God for the victory Jesus has over death and for the opportunity to join with Jesus in resurrection to eternal life.

 OPTIONAL HOMEWORK

1. Draw an image of the vision John sees in **Revelation 1:10-16**.

2. Looking back over your life, think about the most significant moments of joy, pain, celebration, loss, and love to identify how the past has shaped you. Chronicle with a date (even just a year) the most important experiences of your life and add a title or name for the significant experience. Reflect on God's faithfulness in your life and His patience in developing your walk with Him.

_____

_____

_____

_____

_____

_____

_____

_____

_____

_____

_____

_____

_____

_____

_____

_____

_____

_____

3. Begin a journal this week that celebrates the experiences you are having with God each day. Try to be more attentive to God as you participate in this study of the end times.

4. Write down your dreams for the future. What are the desires of your heart that you consistently pray about and discuss with God because they reflect the most important things to you? Which of these emerge from your love for God and love for others, and which dreams emerge from selfish desires or impure motives? As you anticipate the future, analyze what you are hoping to accomplish and whether it's a worthy goal to pursue. After you've identified what is most important to you, talk to God about those things.

 ADDITIONAL RESOURCES

http://www.versebyverseministry.org/videos/revelation-study

Revelation Study: Introduction and Chapter 1

NOTES

NOTES

LESSON 2

The Church Age and the Seven Letters

LEARNING OBJECTIVES: Your goal is to...

1. Discern the purpose of the seven letters;
2. Adopt a lens for understanding the seven letters;
3. And investigate one specific letter that illuminates the others.

PRAYER

Begin your time in prayer by thanking God for good gifts and asking for wisdom and insight during this study. In your quiet time, reflect on the gifts God has given you and how you can use them for God's glory.

REVIEW

1. What framework was offered in Lesson 1 to help us understand the structure of Revelation? How can Revelation be divided?

_____

_____

_____

_____

_____

_____

_____

_____

_____

2. How would you describe the image of Jesus that John saw in **Revelation 1**?

_____

_____

_____

_____

_____

_____

_____

_____

_____

3. What are some of the phrases used in **Revelation 1** to describe God's eternal existence?

_____

_____

_____

_____

_____

_____

_____

_____

_____

_____

_____

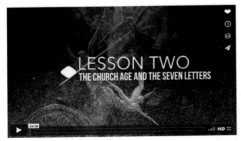

VIDEO 2
The Church Age and the Seven Letters
The Seven Letters (Rev. 2-3)

All videos are available for viewing or download at:
vbvmiendtimesstudy.org

1. How would you summarize the major points from this video?

_____

_____

_____

_____

_____

_____

_____

_____

_____

2. As Pastor Armstrong taught, the letters written to the seven churches comprise a prophecy (even now) concerning the church.

When we compare the order of the letters in Revelation chapters 2 and 3 with their geographic locations, we find a suggestion of chronology. A clockwise pattern emerges that reflects how each letter represents a period of church history over time.

The church had a beginning at Pentecost and will have an end one day (to be discussed later). In between, the church will move through seven periods of time while on the earth. These are the things that are. Furthermore, the number *seven* suggests completeness or the whole of something, indicating that the church will cease after the seventh period is concluded.

Share any reactions or conclusions from your understanding of this unique feature of the seven letters. What are the implications for the church today?

_____

_____

_____

_____

_____

3. Review the three ways to interpret the Bible listed below.

Literal	specific recipients, historical understanding
Universal	general themes, timeless principles
Prophetic	symbolic, speaking about our future

We should always begin by looking at the text *literally*. An important rule of thumb to use when studying the Bible applies here: When the plain sense of Scripture makes common sense, seek no other sense. The commonsense interpretation may not be the most popular understanding or what we personally like. But if the literal interpretation makes sense just as it is, this may very well be the right interpretation.

There are also *universal* truths applicable to many other churches. For example, persecution (Rev. 2:3) and destructive teaching (Rev. 2:15-16) are universally relevant issues churches face.

Sometimes Scripture is *prophetic*. It is symbolic and speaks to our future. This is the case with the seven letters in Revelation 2 and 3.

Can you think of a book of the Bible that matches each type of interpretation?

4. The number seven represents wholeness or completeness in the Bible.

The number *seven* has a certain biblical meaning assigned to it; the idea is complete wholeness, or 100%. For example, God's creative work was completed and finished in seven days. The seven letters can be understood as letters that are written to the *whole* church. Here are a few more examples of the number *seven* representing completion:

> seven days of creation (Gen. 2:1–3)
> seven days Israel marched around Jericho (Josh. 6:4)
> seven times Naaman dipped in the Jordan River to be healed (2 Kings 5:14)
> seven baskets full of pieces collected after 4,000 fed (Mark 8:8)
> seven men selected to resolve an early church conflict (Acts 6:1–6)
> seven golden lampstands (Rev. 1:12)

Why do you think God assigns symbolic meaning to numbers in Scripture in this way?

_____

_____

_____

_____

_____

_____

_____

_____

5. Laodicea was a prosperous, independent city in the Roman Empire. It was a large, commercial banking city known for its black-wool industry (Rev. 3:17–18), medical school (3:17), and eye ointment (3:18). It was also known for its role as the banking center of the region.

"You are neither hot nor cold" (3:15) is a reference to the Laodicea river valley, where river water comes into it from hot sulfuric springs and cold mountain streams.

In AD 60 the city was destroyed by an earthquake but was so independent they rebuilt the city without any assistance from Rome. They were rich and self-reliant. Laodicea means "people ruling" or "judgment of the people."

Why did Jesus draw upon the geographic and cultural features of a city like Laodicea when writing to the church?

APPLICATION

1. Assign one of the first six letters (in Rev. 2 and 3) to individuals or small groups to read and then do the following:

a. Identify what they are *affirmed* for.

b. Identify what they are *confronted* about.

c. Describe what they are *promised*.

2. Compare and contrast the letters to identify themes that are present in the majority of them. In what ways do these letters speak to either you or your church community? Are there any messages the current church needs to hear?

3. If the Spirit were to write you a personal letter, what would you be affirmed for? What would you be confronted about? What would you like to hear God promise?

 **PRAYER**

Thank God for the letters to the churches. Ask God for wisdom this week to view yourself correctly as someone who needs salve to put on your eyes so that you can see (Rev. 3:18).

 OPTIONAL HOMEWORK

1. Read **Acts 19** about Paul's trip to Ephesus and read **Ephesians** to compare them with the letter in **Revelation 2:1-7**. Are there any connections that help you understand more about the city or about the Christians there?

2. Complete the following chart to help you compare and contrast the letters to the churches:

CHURCH	AFFIRMATION	CONFRONTATION	PROMISE
Ephesus			
Smyrna			
Pergamum			
Thyatira			
Sardis			
Philadelphia			
Laodicea			

 ADDITIONAL RESOURCES

http://www.versebyverseministry.org/videos/revelation-study

Revelation Study: Lessons 2A, 2B, 3A, and 3B

NOTES

NOTES

NOTES

LEARNING OBJECTIVES: Your goal is to...

1. Identify connections between Laodicea and the church today;
2. Consider your individual relationship with God through Jesus;
3. And feel renewed urgency to seek the world for God.

PRAYER

Ask God for humility to learn from the Bible and wisdom to hear the message of the Spirit to the churches.

REVIEW

1. What is the relationship between the seven letters to the churches and the church age?

_____

_____

_____

_____

_____

_____

_____

_____

_____

_____

2. In what ways does the letter to Laodicea connect to the geographical and political realities of the time the letter was written?

VIDEO 3

The Great Apostasy
The Great Apostasy (Rev. 3; 2 Thess. 2; 1 Tim. 4; 2 Tim. 3)

All videos are available for viewing or download at:
vbvmiendtimesstudy.org

1. How does the description of the Laodicean church also describe people in churches today?

_____

_____

_____

_____

_____

_____

_____

_____

_____

_____

2. Consider the contrast in **Revelation 3:17**. The Laodicean church says they are rich, wealthy, and in need of nothing, but in reality they are wretched, miserable, poor, blind, and naked. In what ways might the church deceive itself by thinking that it is healthy when in fact it desperately needs healing?

_____

_____

_____

_____

_____

_____

_____

3. Read **Revelation 3:18**. The Spirit offers white garments for the Laodiceans to wear. White garments appear again in **Revelation 6:11, 7:13-14,** and **19:8**, where it says, "Fine linen, bright and clean… stands for the righteous acts of God's people." How do these images relate to being "clothed with Christ" (Gal. 3:27; Rom. 13:14)? What are some specific actions we can take to clothe ourselves with Christ?

4. What are the differences between the visible and the invisible church?

5. The true church is a subset of the whole. Proportionally, during the time of the church of Laodicea, the true, faithful followers of Jesus will become fewer in number. This is the time of the great apostasy.

2 Thessalonians 2:1-3 and **1 Timothy 4:1-3** describe a time when there is a falling away within the larger setting of those who call themselves the church.

Paul says the apostasy (a falling away) comes first, before the end. Paul is not talking about individual Christians ceasing to be Christian here. He is talking about the community changing from one that is mostly Christian to one that is less and less Christian.

Explain *the great apostasy* in your own words. Why do you suppose the Lord allows this to come upon the church in the last days? How is knowing about the great apostasy important to our understanding of prophecy?

6. Read **2 Timothy 3:1-5**. In what ways does this describe our context and culture today?

7. The seventh age, or time period, of the church coincides with the rise of democracy. Historically, this is a unique time because never before have so many countries been ruled democratically by their own people. How do you understand this connection between the letter to Laodicea and the church today?

APPLICATION

1. Knowing we are living in the end times, we should evaluate our relationship with Jesus and what we believe about Him. Describe your foundational beliefs about Jesus.

2. Our present age is a time when all men and women have opportunity to encounter Jesus and know Him, but the age will end soon. Have you gained a greater sense of urgency from understanding the Bible's teaching on our age and times? How does knowing this impact the way you want to serve Jesus and His people?

 PRAYER

Thank God for giving us another day to live on earth, to live in relationship with Him, and to live in relationship with one another. Ask God for a healthy view of time and a sober realization of how short life is.

OPTIONAL HOMEWORK

1. Read **Ecclesiastes 3:1–22**. How does this offer perspective for life?

2. Reflect on the brevity of your life and write out a list of prophetic truths you want to remember when you get caught up in distractions of life.

ADDITIONAL RESOURCES

http://www.versebyverseministry.org/videos/revelation-study

Revelation Study: Lessons 2A, 2B, 3A, and 3B

NOTES

LEARNING OBJECTIVES: Your goal is to...

1. Distinguish between the terms *age* and *last days*;
2. And evaluate how the approach of the end times influences your life.

PRAYER

Ask God for perspective and eyes to see God's activity in history more clearly. Ask for wisdom and the ability to discern what time it is in the chronology of the world.

REVIEW

1. In the last lesson we talked about the ways the letter to Laodicea applied to our context today. What are some ways our culture is like Laodicea?

_____

_____

_____

_____

_____

_____

_____

_____

_____

_____

2. We also talked about the great apostasy. What is this and what does it precede?

_____

_____

_____

_____

_____

_____

_____

_____

_____

_____

_____

_____

_____

_____

VIDEO 4

Understanding God's Timeline
Ages and Last Days

All videos are available for viewing or download at:
vbvmiendtimesstudy.org

1. How would you summarize the primary teaching of this video? What did you learn?

_____

_____

_____

_____

_____

_____

_____

_____

_____

_____

_____

_____

2. An _age_ is a "long but finite time in God's program for creation."
Mark 10:29-30 distinguishes between the _present age_ and the _age to come_. In this age, through faith, we believe that we are receiving an inheritance in the next age. In the age to come we will inherit eternal life.

The _last days_ are a "final period of the current age", which ushers in the next age.
"in the last days difficult times will come" (2 Tim. 3:1)
"in the last days mockers will come" (2 Peter 3:3)

The last days are at the end of the present age and signal that the age to come is approaching. It's like the two-minute warning in sports, alerting everyone that the end is coming.

How does understanding the definition of an _age_ and the definition of _last days_ improve our understanding of prophecy in the Bible? How does it influence the way we live out our faith?

_____

_____

3. Read **Hebrews 1:1-2**. This reframes the length of the present age to extend before the time of the Hebrews writer in the first century. These verses imply that the present age is in the last days of the church age. God was at work long before the existence of the church. How would you retell or summarize the story of God's activity in the world from creation to the present day?

4. The age of the gentiles is defined by three things:
   1. Israel is defeated by gentile powers.
   2. Israel is dispersed into all the nations.
   3. Jerusalem is trampled by the gentiles.

The age of the gentiles began with the Babylonian Empire's King Nebuchadnezzar conquering Israel and overtaking Jerusalem (2 Kings 24-25 and Jer. 52)

Read **Luke 21:24**: "until the times [age] of the gentiles are fulfilled." Understanding the age of the gentiles, in what way is our present age "clocked" by Israel? How does Israel's circumstances in the world help us identify and interpret our own times in relationship to Scripture?

5. In addition to the evidence from Scripture provided, what other evidence suggests we are at the end of the present age, the age of the gentiles?

APPLICATION

1. When people declare that the end of the world is near and then nothing happens, it can lead us to be skeptical or cynical. We may start to wonder if it will ever happen. Have you seen this to be true in your life? Is the end of the world something you think about regularly, or is it something you have dismissed as not likely to happen in your lifetime?

2. As we study the end times, we may be tempted to look forward when there are things to learn by looking backward. There are lessons to establish from history that clarify our perspective on the future in a helpful and necessary way.

Are you more likely to focus on and prepare for the future or to focus on and think about the past? How would a change in perspective (or focus) influence your life?

3. If you sincerely believed that Jesus's return was near, what would you do differently? How would this affect your decisions or how you spend your time?

PRAYER

Thank God for another day of life and the opportunity to learn about the end times. Invite God to convict you about the amount of time you have on earth and to live in response to this awareness.

OPTIONAL HOMEWORK

1. Read **2 Kings 24** and **25**. Chronicle the order of events that led to Israel's Babylonian captivity.

2. Read **Jeremiah 52**. Compare this account of Nebuchadnezzar's reign with 2 Kings, looking for similarities and any new information.

_____

_____

_____

_____

_____

_____

_____

_____

_____

_____

_____

_____

_____

_____

_____

_____

_____

ADDITIONAL RESOURCES

http://www.versebyverseministry.org/videos/revelation-study

Revelation Study: Lesson 4A

NOTES

NOTES

LESSON 5

The Age of the Gentiles (Daniel 2 and 7)

PRAYER

Ask God for wisdom to understand Scripture and for the ability to interpret time from a godly perspective. Reflect on the ways you can use your time to serve in God's kingdom.

REVIEW

1. In the last lesson we defined two terms: *ages* and *last days*. What do these mean?

2. What name did Jesus give for our current age of history? When did it begin?

VIDEO 5

The Age of the Gentiles (Daniel 2 and 7)
Purpose for the Age of Gentiles (Lev. 26; Deut. 29; Deut. 30)

All videos are available for viewing or download at:
vbvmiendtimesstudy.org

DISCUSSION

1. What are some of the major points you learned from the video?

2. How do the features of Nebuchadnezzar's dream of a statue represent a timeline of history called the age of the gentiles?

3. Each part of the statue in **Daniel 2** represents something specific (vv. 31–35).

    1. Head (gold) = Babylon
    2. Chest and arms (silver) = Medo-Persian Empire
    3. Stomach and thighs (bronze) = Greek Empire (Alexander the Great)
    4. Legs (iron) and feet (iron and clay) = Roman Empire (and Imperialistic Democratic Alliances)

How do the details of each section relate to these kingdoms?

4. The four successive kingdoms represented by the statue must meet four criteria. Each must:

     1. be a gentile kingdom;

     2. be the dominant power in the world;

     3. be in possession of Babylon;

     4. and occupy (trample) Jerusalem.

Explain in your own words why these criteria are important. How do they help our interpretation of **Daniel 2**?

5. In **Daniel 2:34-35** Jesus is pictured by the rock uncut by human hands and the mountain that fills the whole earth represents His kingdom. Why do you think the Spirit decided to picture Jesus and His coming kingdom in these particular ways?

6. In what ways does Christ's kingdom "crush" the kingdoms of the earth (Dan. 2:44)?

7. Summarize the main point(s) of **Daniel 2**. Why is this chapter of Scripture so important to understanding prophecy?

APPLICATION

1. How does your understanding of world history (and the temporary nature of earthly kingdoms) influence how you view powerful nations and kingdoms today? Does looking at the past or looking toward the future influence how you see the present kingdoms?

2. Philippians 3:20 says, "our citizenship is in heaven." How should a Christian live under the authority of an earthly kingdom while still hoping for and claiming allegiance to a coming heavenly kingdom? Can you cite any Scripture to support your conclusions?

PRAYER

End with Daniel's prayer to God in **Daniel 2:20-22**:

>   God, may Your name be praised forever and ever.
>   Wisdom and power are yours.
>   You change times and seasons; You set up kings and You remove them.
>   You give wisdom to the wise and You give knowledge to the discerning.
>   You reveal deep and hidden things; You know what lies in darkness,
>   And light dwells with You. Thank You for all of your gifts. We pray in Jesus'
>   name. Amen.

OPTIONAL HOMEWORK

1. Read **Daniel chapter 2**. Diagram the statue and the interpretation of the dream in **Daniel 2:36-45**.

2. Read **Exodus 31:18, 32:15-19**; and **34:1** describing the stone tablets of the Law. Read **Exodus 20:25** explaining that altars were to be built with uncut stones. Read **1 Peter 2:4-8** describing Jesus as a rejected but essential stone that causes some to fall.

How many of these features of Jesus can you find in the "stone" of **Daniel 2**?

_____

_____

_____

_____

_____

_____

_____

_____

_____

_____

_____

_____

_____

 ADDITIONAL RESOURCES

http://www.versebyverseministry.org/videos/revelation-study

Revelation Study: Lesson 4B

NOTES

LEARNING OBJECTIVES: Your goal is to...

1. Identify how Daniel's vision helps interpret and explain Nebuchadnezzar's dream;
2. Understand God's consistent work throughout history, which is approaching completion;
3. And feel a sense of urgency about the approaching end times.

PRAYER

As Gabriel appeared to Daniel to give him "insight and understanding" (Dan. 9:22), ask God to provide insight and understanding as you study His Word.

REVIEW

1. What do each of the parts of the statue in **Daniel 2** represent (Dan. 2:31–35)?

_____

_____

_____

_____

_____

_____

_____

_____

_____

_____

_____

_____

2. What do the rock (not cut by human hands) and the mountain filling the whole earth represent in **Daniel 2:34-35**?

_____

_____

_____

_____

_____

_____

_____

_____

_____

_____

_____

_____

_____

VIDEO 6

The Seventy Sevens (Daniel 9)
The Final Seven

All videos are available for viewing or download at:
vbvmiendtimesstudy.org

1. What is the most memorable detail of the video to you?

2. How does **Daniel 7** correspond to **Daniel 2**? How are the dreams of Nebuchadnezzar and Daniel "two sides of the same coin"? How are they related?

3. Read **Daniel 7:1-8** and **7:19-27** and consult the table below. What new information are we learning about the kingdoms beyond what we learned in **Daniel 2**? What is the main focus of this chapter?

Daniel 2	Kingdoms	Daniel 7
Head	Babylonians	Lion
Chest and Arms	Medo-Persians	Bear
Stomach and Thighs	Greeks	Leopard
Legs and Feet	Romans (Imperialistic Democratic Alliances)	Beast with ten horns

4. Read **Deuteronomy 29:9-15**. The old covenant was established with all future generations of Israel. This was not an individual covenant. It was a national covenant that Israel as a group is bound to.

Why does the age of the gentiles exist?

_____

_____

_____

_____

_____

_____

_____

_____

_____

_____

5. Read **Leviticus 26:2-4** and **Leviticus 26:14-16**. How do these verses predict the consequences that occurred to Israel?

_____

_____

_____

_____

_____

_____

_____

_____

_____

6. Read **Leviticus 26:40-45**.

A "loophole" in the old covenant permits the nation of Israel to receive the blessings in another way, but a national confession of faith is required.

7. Read the following summary of this lesson and discuss anything that may be unclear in your group. This is an important conclusion in this study, so don't move beyond this point if you are confused. Rewatch the video for Lesson 6 if necessary.

- The old covenant requires perfect obedience to the Law by all generations of Israel.
- Failure to perfectly keep the Law results in the curses of the Law.
- The age of the gentiles is the fulfillment of the curses against Israel.
- One day Israel will confess Christ and receive the blessings of the kingdom on the basis of the Abrahamic covenant.

Outline of **Daniel 9**
9:1-3	Daniel's Mistake
9:4-19	Daniel's Prayer
9:20-23	Gabriel's Rebuke

The purpose of the seventy sevens (Dan. 58:20) is for Israel and Jerusalem to:
1. finish the transgression;
2. make an end of sin;
3. atone for Israel's sin;
4. bring everlasting righteousness;
5. seal up prophecy;
6. and anoint the temple.

Daniel's seventy sevens (of Dan. 9) is the age of the gentiles and will last 490 years.

APPLICATION

1. The kingdoms described in the dreams of the statue and the beast are all kingdoms that rise to power and then pass away as others take over. How does that influence your view of the current powerful kingdoms (nations) on earth? Do you believe those in power now might one day be out of power?

2. Read **Romans 11:25-29**. God put a pause in the clock so that the gentiles could come to know Christ and God. How does this align with the Great Commission given by Jesus to His disciples in **Matthew 28:19-20**?

PRAYER

End with Daniel's prayer in **Daniel 9:4**; "Lord, You are the great and awesome God who keeps your covenant of love with those who love You and keep Your commandments." Help me to love like You love and help me to follow Your instructions for living. Please forgive me when I sin and help me to respond to what I have learned.

 OPTIONAL HOMEWORK

1. Read **2 Peter 3:8-18**. What is the reason for God's patience?

2. Make a list of the commands in these verses that are given in light of the coming day of the Lord. (See **2 Peter 3:11-12, 14, 17**.)

✚ ADDITIONAL RESOURCES

http://www.versebyverseministry.org/videos/revelation-study

Revelation Study: Lessons 4C and 13

NOTES

NOTES

LEARNING OBJECTIVES: Your goal is to...

1. Explain the position of the church within the age of the gentiles;
2. Describe the events that will precede the end times;
3. And identify evidence for the approaching end times.

PRAYER

Thank You for the body of Christ, Your church, and for the messages You've sent us in your Word, the Bible. May we continue to pursue knowledge and insight from the Bible as we seek Your truth to teach us how to live.

REVIEW

1. How are Nebuchadnezzar's dream in **Daniel 2** and Daniel's dream in **Daniel 7** related?

2. What are the seventy sevens discussed in **Daniel 9**?

_____

_____

_____

_____

_____

_____

_____

_____

_____

_____

_____

_____

VIDEO 7

Signs of the Times
Events Prior to Daniel's Final Seven

All videos are available for viewing or download at:
vbvmiendtimesstudy.org

DISCUSSION

1. How did the review in the video help summarize what we've been learning?

_____

_____

_____

_____

_____

_____

_____

_____

_____

_____

2. Where does the church fall in the larger timeline of this present age (the age of the gentiles) and what event concludes this age? How does this change or enhance your understanding of the end times?

_____

_____

_____

_____

_____

_____

_____

_____

_____

_____

_____

_____

_____

3. The Lord pauses Israel's 490-year judgment so the gentile church has opportunity to receive the gospel. What promise did the Lord make that obligated Him to make this opportunity available for gentiles?

4. What happens after the current "pause" ends and the countdown of the 490-year period resumes?

5. Review the following:

- Church apostasy (Rev. 3; 1 Tim. 4:1-3; 2 Thess. 2:3)
  The apostasy will happen first.
- Regathering Israel (Ezek. 20 and 22)
  After Israel is scattered, they will be gathered again into their land.
- Emergence of ten world rulers (Dan. 2 and 7)
  These rulers have not yet emerged.
- Return of Elijah to prepare Israel (Mal. 4:4-6)
  Elijah will return to restore the hearts of people to their ancestors.
  Israel will return to a temple and sacrifice at it (becoming Orthodox again).
- Resurrection of the bride of Christ (1 Thess. 1:10; 1 Thess. 5:9)

  Only the first two have occurred. The beginning of the end is beginning to happen now.

None of these events had occurred until the turn of the twentieth century, but now they are being fulfilled. How does this pattern change your appreciation for the days in which you live?

_____

_____

_____

_____

_____

_____

_____

6. What evidence do you see that indicates to you the end is approaching?

_____

_____

_____

_____

_____

_____

APPLICATION

1. What are the ways a person who believes that the end times are coming will live differently than a person who believes the earth will continue forever?

2. What responsibility do Christians have to remind each other of the approaching end?

3. Does knowing about the end of the age comfort you as a Christian or cause concern? Why?

_____

_____

_____

_____

_____

_____

_____

_____

_____

_____

_____

_____

_____

_____

_____

_____

_____

_____

PRAYER

Ask God to give you the vision to see the signs of the times and respond appropriately.

1. Read **Matthew 16:1-3**. What point was Jesus trying to make to the Pharisees? How might we apply it to people today?

2. Write out a "spiritual forecast" for the church and the world based on the things you've learned so far.

ADDITIONAL RESOURCES

http://www.versebyverseministry.org/videos/revelation-study

Revelation Study: Lesson 5D

NOTES

LESSON 8

The End of the Age

LEARNING OBJECTIVES: Your goal is to...

1. List signs of the end of the age from the Olivet Discourse;
2. Chronicle how Matthew and Luke record Jesus's responses to the apostles' questions;
3. And evaluate the signs and your relationship to the approaching end times.

PRAYER

Ask God to help you be open to the ways He is working in the world. Ask God for the vision to see by faith and not just by sight, because through faith we believe that Jesus is returning soon.

REVIEW

1. List some events Jesus said will precede the end of the age.

2. What additional evidence suggests the end is approaching?

_____

_____

_____

_____

_____

_____

_____

_____

_____

_____

_____

_____

_____

VIDEO 8

The End of the Age
Signs of the End of the Age
(Olivet Discourse—Matt. 24)

All videos are available for viewing or
download at:
vbvmiendtimesstudy.org

1. What point(s) in the videos were most noteworthy to you?

_____

_____

_____

_____

_____

_____

_____

_____

_____

_____

2. Compare and contrast **Matthew 24** and **Luke 21** by reading the following sections:

	Apostles' Questions	Asked	Answered in Matthew	Answered in Luke
1.	When?	Matt. 24:3; Luke 21:7		21:12-19
1a.	Signs it's about to happen?	Luke 21:7		21:24
2.	Signs of Your coming?	Matt. 24:3	24:9, 27-29	21:12, 25
3.	Signs of the end of the age?	Matt. 24:3	24:7-8	21:10-11
4.	What are not signs?		24:4-6	

Apostles' questions on hearing that the temple will be torn down (Matt. 24:3 and Luke 21:7):

1. When will these things (the temple's destruction) happen?
1a. What will be signs when these things are about to take place (Luke 21:7)?
2. What will be the signs of Your coming?
3. What will be the signs of the end of the age?

Jesus answers in this order (Matt. 24:4-6 and Luke 21:8-9):
4. Jesus answers with things that are not signs we are near the end, such as wars.
3. Wars, famines, and earthquakes are the beginnings of an increase in severity and frequency of pain prior to the end, which is a birth of new life (Matt. 24:7-8).
1. and 1a. Persecution will occur (Luke 21:12-19, 24).
2. At the second coming there will be darkness. (Matt. 24:29; Luke 21:25).

3. Read **Matthew 24:4-14**. What are some of the signs Jesus lists to identify when the end is approaching?

4. How do we know that the two world wars of the twentieth century confirm we are nearing the end of this age? What made them unique wars?

_____

_____

_____

_____

_____

_____

_____

_____

_____

5. How does the dramatic increase in earthquakes from years 2000 to 2010 influence your belief that the end is near?

_____

_____

_____

_____

_____

_____

_____

_____

_____

_____

6. Do you view the famines of the world in a similar way to earthquakes? In your mind, do they point to the end times?

7. What event(s) would have to happen before you started to believe the end was near?

APPLICATION

1. The apostles were impressed with the massive stones and the structure of the physical temple while Jesus saw them for what they were going to become: a pile of rubble. What physical (and social) structures are we sometimes tempted to admire whose future is less certain than our own? (Are there any cultural objects or rules that you're offering an excess of admiration?)

2. If you were convinced that the end was approaching before the end of this year, what allegiances would you change? How would you spend your time differently?

PRAYER

Ask God to give you the wisdom to choose wisely whom you are committed to and whom you have allegiance to. Ask God for the vision to see the structures of the world with eyes of faith beyond our present time so that everything is seen with a godly perspective.

OPTIONAL HOMEWORK

1. Read **1 Peter**. Describe some of the ways Christians can expect to be persecuted for their faith. (See especially 1:6, 2:21-23, 3:8-18, 4:12-19.)

ADDITIONAL RESOURCES

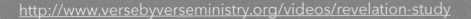
http://www.versebyverseministry.org/videos/revelation-study

Revelation Study: Lessons 5D, 5E, and 6A

NOTES

LEARNING OBJECTIVES: Your goal is to...

1. Distinguish between the *coming of the Lord* and the *day of the Lord*;
2. Identify similarities between the Jewish wedding tradition and the return of Jesus;
3. And commit to specific actions this week that help you prepare for Christ's return.

PRAYER

Thank God for the knowledge of the approaching end times. Thank God for the promise and hope of salvation. Ask God for the wisdom to know how to live in light of the coming end.

REVIEW

1. Matthew 24 and **Luke 21** both retell the Olivet Discourse speech made by Jesus. What are the main points of this speech?

_____

_____

_____

_____

_____

_____

_____

_____

_____

_____

_____

2. What are some of the signs listed in the last lesson that signal the end is approaching?

> See **Matthew 24:4-14**:
> World wars
> Increase in earthquakes
> Increase in famines
> Tribulation
> Signs in the heavens
> Persecution

VIDEO 9

**The Resurrection of the Bride
(Rev. 4–5; 1 Thess. 1, 5; 1 Cor. 15)**
The Jewish Wedding Tradition

All videos are available for viewing or download at:
vbvmiendtimesstudy.org

1. Summarize the main points you learned in the video.

_____

_____

_____

_____

_____

_____

_____

_____

_____

_____

2. Read **1 Thessalonians 5:2-4** and **2 Peter 3:9-10**. Who will experience the day of the Lord, according to Paul and Peter?

_____

_____

_____

_____

_____

_____

_____

_____

_____

_____

_____

It is not for believers but for the "they" (unbelievers) Paul writes about in **1 Thessalonians 5:2-4** and which is written about in **2 Peter 3:9-10**.

3. Review the list of other names the Bible gives for this same day.

> "great and terrible day of the Lord" (Mal. 4)
> "tribulation" (Deut. 4:30)
> "the time of Jacob's troubles" (Jer. 30:7)
> "the indignation" (Dan. 11:36)
> "the day of vengeance" (Isa. 34:8)
> "the day of wrath" (Zeph. 1:15)
> "the year of recompense" (Isa. 34:8)
> "the day of darkness" (Joel 2:2)
> "the day of Jehovah" (Joel 1:15)

The *day of the Lord* always means tribulation. It is not the second coming of Christ. It is the period of the seven years that remain in Daniel's seventy sevens and is a period of great destruction.

What do you learn about this day simply by its various names?

4. Review the Bible's teaching on the coming of the Lord.

> "You are our hope, joy, and crown when Jesus comes" (1 Thess. 2:19, 20).
> "Be patient until the coming of the Lord, which is near. The judge is at the door" (James 5:7-9).
> "Don't judge before the appointed time. Wait until the Lord comes" (1 Cor. 4:5).
> "Jesus will come at an unexpected hour" (Matt. 24:44).

List some of the characteristics of this "day." What stands out?

_____

_____

_____

_____

_____

_____

_____

5. Read **2 Thessalonians 2:1-4**. How would you describe the differences between the *coming of the Lord* and the *day of the Lord*?

_____

_____

_____

_____

_____

_____

_____

_____

6. Review the features of the throne room in **Revelation 4** and **5**.

Twenty-four elders = human leaders
White robes = believers in Christ
Wearing crowns = rewarded for service

The seven spirits of God are also present. (See Isa. 11:2.) In other words, the entire (whole) spirit of God is present.

What conclusions do you draw from the scene?

7. Read **John 14:2-3**. In the video, we learned that:

Jesus is going to heaven (the Father's house) to prepare dwelling places. If Jesus goes, He will return to receive people to Himself, where He is in heaven.

This is distinct from the second coming, because at the second coming Jesus comes to the earth and stays. The coming of the Lord is called "the resurrection of the bride" in **1 Corinthians 15:51-53**.

Why do you think Jesus gave the disciples this promise? What purpose would it serve in the lives of all believers?

_____

_____

_____

_____

_____

_____

_____

8. Read **1 Thessalonians 4:13-18** and **1 Corinthians 15:51-53**.
The resurrection of the church from the earth ends the church age and opens the door for the final events of the age of the gentiles. In what ways will the sudden removal of the church likely affect the world?

_____

_____

_____

_____

_____

_____

_____

9. Review the following reason for the coming of tribulation upon Israel and the earth.

     1. Daniel's seventieth week is intended for unbelieving Israel (Dan. 9).
     2. The bride of Christ is not appointed for wrath (1 Thess. 5).
     3. The bride's home has been made ready (John 14:2-3).
     4. The complete number of gentiles has been reached (Rom. 11:25).
     5. The entire bride must be collected in the same moment
(1 Cor. 15; Heb. 11-12).

What would you say to Christians who worry about experiencing some or all of the tribulation?

10. When is the coming of the Lord (Matt. 24:36-37)?

APPLICATION

1. How does the Jewish wedding tradition inform your understanding of the end times?

2. How does the need for the bride to be prepared and spotless relate to our preparation for Christ's return? What could you do today to prepare for Christ's return?

PRAYER

Thank God for the words of Scripture that reveal the truth about time and that we are moving toward the return of Jesus. Ask God to help you prepare your heart and your life for that return.

OPTIONAL HOMEWORK

1. Read **Matthew 25:1-13**. How does this story of attendants at a Jewish wedding contribute to your understanding of the second coming?

2. What are the characteristics of people who are prepared for the groom to return at any time? How can we be among those people?

_____

_____

_____

_____

_____

_____

_____

_____

_____

_____

_____

_____

_____

_____

_____

ADDITIONAL RESOURCES

http://www.versebyverseministry.org/videos/revelation-study

Revelation Study: Lessons 5A, 5B, 5C, and 19A

NOTES

LEARNING OBJECTIVES: Your goal is to...

1. Identify miracles that distinguish the Messiah's work from other miracle workers in Israel;
2. Describe how Jesus's work casting out demons was distinct from other exorcisms;
3. And define blasphemy and explain the unforgivable sin.

PRAYER

Thank God for the power of His Word and the ways it is living and active in our hearts and lives. Invite God to help you grow in the grace and knowledge of our Lord Jesus Christ.

REVIEW

1. What is the difference between the *day of the Lord* and the *coming of the Lord*?

2. How does the Jewish wedding tradition contribute to our understanding of the coming of the Lord?

_____

_____

_____

_____

_____

_____

_____

_____

_____

_____

_____

_____

_____

VIDEO 10

The Departure of Christ
The Reason for Jesus's Departure (Luke 13); The Messianic Miracle; The Unforgivable Sin

All videos are available for viewing or download at:
vbvmiendtimesstudy.org

DISCUSSION

1. What do you understand in a new way because of the video?

2. What are the first two (of three) events that precede the end?

3. What period of history is concluded with the coming of the rock from heaven? What period of history follows?

_____

_____

_____

_____

_____

_____

_____

_____

_____

_____

_____

_____

_____

_____

_____

_____

_____

_____

_____

_____

4. Review what we learned about miracles.

Many miracles happened in Israel during the Old Testament period:
Healing (2 Kings 5)
Raising from the dead (1 Kings 17)
Exorcisms (Mark 9)

Some other miracles were specific to the Messiah:
Healing a Jew of leprosy (Matt. 8; Mark 1; Luke 5 and 17)
Healing a man born blind (John 9)
Exorcising a mute demon (Matt. 12; Luke 13)

Why do you think the Lord reserved certain miracles for His Son? Though Messianic miracles are not specifically called out in Scripture, what can we see in Scripture that tells us such a thing truly exists?

5. Review what we learned about Jewish exorcisms.

1. Jewish men empowered by the Spirit could cast out demons from bodies.
There were "Jewish exorcists" (Acts 19:11-16).

2. They had to follow a prescribed method.
Exorcists would ask the name of the demon because they had to cast it out by name (Luke 8:26-31).

3. God set limits of their power to reserve a miracle for the Messiah.
Only the Messiah would be able to exorcise a demon from a mute person, from whom no one could learn the name of the demon (Mark 9:17-19, 25-29).

Before you watched the video, did an exorcism seem like fact or fiction to you? What does this say about the influence of modern media and entertainment on our attitudes toward spiritual matters?

6. Read **Matthew 12:22-23**. How does the crowd's reaction suggest they thought this miracle was unique to the Messiah?

_____

_____

_____

_____

_____

_____

_____

_____

_____

_____

7. Read **Matthew 12:13-32**. When the Pharisees attributed Jesus's work to the work of Satan, they were saying the work of the Holy Spirit was from Satan. This is the unforgivable sin.

Blasphemy is not only claiming to be God or be from God when you are not. Blasphemy is also the opposite, denying that what is from God is from God.

In this case, the Pharisees say the work of the Holy Spirit is from Satan. The unforgivable sin was a one-time event: Israel's rejection of Jesus, who was God in human form and performed miracles by the Spirit. Instead, they called His miracles the work of Satan.

Today, there is no unforgivable sin. Every sin is forgivable by the blood of Christ when we repent and turn to Christ in faith.

In your own words, explain why the unforgivable sin can't be committed today.

_____

_____

_____

_____

_____

APPLICATION

1. One definition of blasphemy is failure to attribute God's work to God, but instead to say it is fueled by some other power. How can you be more open to the work of God in the world? In what areas of your life are you skeptical of God's working or God's ability to work?

_____

_____

_____

_____

_____

_____

_____

_____

_____

_____

_____

_____

_____

_____

_____

_____

_____

_____

_____

_____

_____

2. By what standards can you evaluate whether something is from God or not? Read **Matthew 7:15-20** and **12:33**. How do these verses teach us to recognize who and what is from God?

_____

_____

_____

_____

_____

_____

_____

_____

_____

_____

_____

_____

_____

_____

_____

_____

_____

_____

 PRAYER

Ask God to give you the faith to believe in the Spirit's work throughout the Bible and among us today. Ask God to help you see and proclaim God's goodness through events in your life.

OPTIONAL HOMEWORK

1. Spend one day chronicling the works of God around and within you. You might write these all down in one place. Thank God for blessings and pray that you can identify the evidence of God's spirit working.

2. Devote a day to intentionally forgiving others who have wronged you. Spend the day thanking God for His forgiveness and asking for His power to help you forgive others. See **Matthew 6:12, 14-15**: "And forgive us our debts as we forgive our debtors… For if you forgive other people when they sin against you, your heavenly Father will also forgive you. But if you do not forgive others their sin, your Father will not forgive your sins."

ADDITIONAL RESOURCES

http://www.versebyverseministry.org/videos/revelation-study

Revelation Study: Lesson 19

NOTES

LESSON 11

The Return of Christ

LEARNING OBJECTIVES: Your goal is to...

1. Summarize the events leading to the need for Israel to have a national confession of faith;
2. Describe the consequence for Israel's refusal to believe in Jesus as the Messiah;
3. And evaluate the power of proclaiming Jesus's identity as God's Son, the Messiah.

PRAYER

Invite God to continue His work today through your community and through studying His Word together.

REVIEW

1. Why does Jesus healing a demon-possessed man who was blind and mute signal that He was the Messiah?

_____

_____

_____

_____

_____

_____

_____

_____

_____

_____

2. What is blasphemy, and what is the unforgivable sin?

_____

_____

_____

_____

_____

_____

_____

_____

_____

_____

_____

_____

VIDEO 11

The Return of Christ
The Covenants with Israel

All videos are available for viewing or download at:
vbvmiendtimesstudy.org

1. How did the video help you understand the topic in a new way?

2. Read **Matthew 12:38-40**. What was the only sign Jesus offered to the Pharisees and teachers of the Law who requested a sign? What do you think Jesus meant by this sign?

3. Review the following comparison of the first and second halves of the Gospel of Matthew.

Matthew 1-12	Matthew 13-28
Jesus spoke openly	Taught parables only
Miracles for all	Faith required
Declared kingdom openly	Ordered, "Tell no one"
Taught everyone	Prepared disciples only

What reason did Jesus have for these changes?

_____

_____

_____

_____

_____

_____

_____

_____

_____

_____

_____

_____

_____

_____

_____

_____

_____

4. Read **Luke 13:34-35**. Jesus withdrew His offer of the kingdom from that generation of Israel, and He chose instead to focus on teaching His disciples.

What reasons do you suppose Jesus had for continuing His earthly ministry for several years after withdrawing the offer of the kingdom?

_____

_____

_____

_____

_____

_____

_____

_____

_____

_____

_____

_____

5. Look through **Psalm 118** briefly. You'll notice this is a messianic psalm that foretold the coming of the Messiah for Israel. **Psalm 118:26** says "Blessed is He who comes in the name of the Lord."

In **Luke 19:37-40** some in Israel sang this psalm as Jesus entered Jerusalem on Palm Sunday, which was the Sunday before He died.
Because not **all** Israel affirmed Jesus's identity on that day, this prophecy remains unfulfilled.

Those few in Israel who declared the fulfillment of Psalm 118 on Palm Sunday were acting in faith, yet not in God's timing. Can you think of times when you acted in faith but were ahead of God's timing? How does knowing this change your approach to following God?

_____

_____

_____

_____

_____

6. What is the connection between a national confession of faith by Israel and the return of Christ?

7. Review the following summary of how Israel reaches the point of a national confession:

> 1. The Messiah came to Israel as promised.
> 2. Israel, through their leaders, rejected their Messiah and committed the unforgivable sin.
> 3. Jesus then withdrew the kingdom offer from Israel for that generation.
> 4. A future generation must call on His name before Jesus returns to set up the kingdom.

What factors contribute to Israel making such a confession? What is the most important factor?

8. Read **Leviticus 26:40-42**. How will a national confession by Israel result in their reconciliation with God?

APPLICATION

1. In what ways does our own personal confession of Christ's identity as God's Son, the Messiah, have power? Why is it important for disciples of Jesus to proclaim His identity?

2. What are some of the small ways we reject the identity of Jesus through our actions? What would you be willing to commit to doing this week to proclaim the lordship of Jesus through your actions?

PRAYER

Ask God to give you the courage and faith to proclaim that Jesus is Christ, both with your mouth and with your life.

 OPTIONAL HOMEWORK

1. Consider the following confessions of faith in Jesus. List who said them and what they said:

Scripture	Who confesses Jesus	What the person says
Mark 8:29		
Mark 15:39		
John 11:24–27		

2. Where in the New Testament are other examples of confessing faith in Jesus?

_____

_____

_____

_____

_____

_____

_____

_____

3. Read the Apostles' Creed as a confession of faith in Christ.

I believe in God, the Father almighty,
　　creator of heaven and earth.
I believe in Jesus Christ, His only Son, our Lord,
　　who was conceived by the Holy Spirit
　　and born of the virgin Mary.
　　He suffered under Pontius Pilate,
　　was crucified, died, and was buried;
　　He descended to hell.
　　The third day He rose again from the dead.
　　He ascended to heaven
　　and is seated at the right hand of God the Father almighty.
　　From there he will come to judge the living and the dead.
I believe in the Holy Spirit,
　　the holy catholic* church,
　　the communion of saints,
　　the forgiveness of sins,
　　the resurrection of the body,
　　and the life everlasting. Amen.

ADDITIONAL RESOURCES

http://www.versebyverseministry.org/videos/revelation-study

Revelation Study: Lessons 20A, 20B, and 20D

NOTES

NOTES

LEARNING OBJECTIVES: Your goal is to...

1. Describe the ways Armageddon leads Israel to repentance;
2. Explain how the national confession by all of Israel results in their salvation;
3. And identify specific goals for future study of this topic, personal preparation for Jesus's return, or sharing this information with others.

PRAYER

Thank God for the promise of the return of His Son, Jesus. Ask God for the vision to look forward to this event with anticipation.

REVIEW

1. What factors contribute to Israel making such a confession? What is the most important factor?

2. How will a national confession of faith lead Israel to reconciliation with God?

_____

_____

_____

_____

_____

_____

_____

_____

_____

_____

_____

_____

_____

_____

VIDEO 12

The Saving of Israel
Armageddon; The Saving of Israel

All videos are available for viewing or download at:
vbvmiendtimesstudy.org

1. How would you summarize the primary teaching of the video?

_____

_____

_____

_____

_____

_____

_____

_____

_____

_____

2. What does the tribulation that happens in the final seven years lead Israel to do?

_____

_____

_____

_____

_____

_____

_____

_____

_____

_____

_____

According to **Daniel 9:24** the seventy sevens were decreed so that Israel would come to repentance and a national confession. They will eventually call on Jesus.

3. Read through the following passages of Scripture. Summarize the Bible's teaching on the war of Armageddon and how it arrives at Israel's repentance.

Nations attack Jerusalem from the west (Joel 3:11-13).
The Lord draws Israel's enemies into battle for destruction (Zech. 12:8-9).
God defends the people in Jerusalem against the enemy (Zech. 12:2-5).
God orchestrates the battle to refine and test Israel (Zech. 13:7-9).
The battle rages three days (Hos. 6:1-3).
Israel will earnestly seek God (Hos. 5:15).
The Spirit is poured out on Jerusalem as they mourn and repent (Zech. 12:10).

4. How is Israel's moment of conversion emotionally different from most people's conversions? Read **Zechariah 12:11-14.**

5. Whom do the groups mentioned in **Zechariah 12:11-14** represent?

6. Read **2 Samuel 16:5-11** and **2 Samuel 19:16-23**. In the video you learned that Shimei's experiences picture future things for certain groups in Israel, both at Jesus's first coming and His second coming. Explain in your own words whom he pictures.

7. How does the story of Shimei point to a national confession of all Israel?

_____

_____

_____

_____

_____

_____

_____

_____

_____

_____

_____

8. Read **Romans 11:25-29.** How do these verses help you understand the end times (i.e., "All Israel will be saved" [v. 26])?

_____

_____

_____

_____

_____

_____

_____

_____

9. Read **Revelation 19:11-16**. The armies of heaven are on white horses and wearing white linen. Whom does this represent?

10. Read **Zechariah 14:2-5**. How is Israel delivered from the nations waging war against them?

APPLICATION

1. If you were going to continue studying this topic, what are some specific goals you would set for yourself?

_____

_____

_____

_____

_____

_____

_____

_____

_____

_____

_____

_____

_____

2. What are some personal actions of preparation you could make for Jesus's return?

_____

_____

_____

_____

_____

_____

_____

_____

_____

_____

_____

3. In what context or with whom might you share what you've learned in this study?

_____

_____

_____

_____

_____

_____

_____

_____

_____

_____

_____

 PRAYER

Ask God to give you a sense of urgency about the return of His Son, Jesus. Ask Him also to give you the passion to continue thinking about and studying the end times and sharing the truth about these things with others.

OPTIONAL HOMEWORK

1. Read **Revelation 22.** Create a message for yourself that reminds you Jesus is coming soon. Place this somewhere you will see it daily.

ADDITIONAL RESOURCES

http://www.versebyverseministry.org/videos/revelation-study

Revelation Study: Lessons 16, 17, 18, 19A, 19B, 19C, and 21/22

NOTES

NOTES

NOTES

Made in the USA
Monee, IL
14 March 2023

29827234R00093